United States Government Accountability Office

Report to the Ranking Member, Committee on Environment and Public Works, U.S. Senate

I0448779

June 2013

U.S. ARMY CORPS OF ENGINEERS

Building Overhead Costs into Projects and Customers' Views on Information Provided

June 2013

GAO Highlights

Highlights of GAO-13-528, a report to the Ranking Member, Committee on Environment and Public Works, U.S. Senate

U.S. ARMY CORPS OF ENGINEERS

Building Overhead Costs into Projects and Customers' Views on Information Provided

Why GAO Did This Study

The Corps spends billions of dollars annually on projects in its Civil Works program. Part of the cost of doing business with the Corps involves paying for overhead—costs that do not directly relate to a specific project or activity but more generally support agency operations. Overhead costs are included in the amount that Congress appropriates for specific Corps projects and the amount that customers pay for Corps' services. The Corps provides services to customers including other Department of Defense units, federal agencies, state and local governments, Indian tribes, and foreign governments. The Corps' Civil Works program is organized around its headquarters, 8 divisions, and 38 districts nationwide. Only district overhead is charged to projects; overhead for headquarters and divisions is not.

You asked GAO to review the Corps' process for building overhead costs into projects. This report examines (1) how the Corps builds overhead costs into its projects and (2) customers' views on overhead information. To accomplish this, GAO reviewed Corps' documentation of its overhead and billing processes, interviewed officials at Corps headquarters, 2 divisions, and 4 districts based on geographic location, and interviewed 16 of the highest paying federal and nonfederal Corps' customers in fiscal year 2012. The results of these interviews cannot be generalized to all customers but provided insights.

GAO is not making recommendations in this report. The Department of Defense did not provide comments.

View GAO-13-528. For more information, contact Anne-Marie Fennell at (202) 512-3841 or fennella@gao.gov.

What GAO Found

The U.S. Army Corps of Engineers (Corps) uses a multistep process to build overhead costs into projects. At the foundation of this process, Corps policy establishes two categories of costs to calculate overhead—general and administrative overhead expenses associated with district administrative offices, such as resource management, and technical overhead expenses associated with district technical offices, such as engineering. Using these two categories as a starting point, the Corps next calculates overhead rates as part of its annual budget process. Specifically, each district administrative and technical office develops operating budgets with overhead estimates, which are then consolidated and routed through district and division management, resulting in a final division-wide operating budget and overhead rates. The Corps then bills projects for overhead costs based on the number of hours its staff charge to projects. Overhead charges are not applied to hours worked by contracted labor, which represent a substantial amount of work. The Corps reports that it contracts out most of its design work and all of its construction work to private sector entities, such as architectural and engineering firms and construction companies. Finally, the Corps periodically monitors overhead costs and makes any necessary adjustments such as changing overhead rates, reducing expenditures, or providing rebates to customers. The Corps is able to monitor overhead because it tracks overhead costs separately from other project costs in its financial management system through specific overhead accounting codes.

Corps customers' views varied on whether overhead information is accessible and understandable. Half of the 16 highest paying customers GAO interviewed said overhead information is generally accessible and understandable. For example, one federal customer said that the Corps provides overhead information in monthly bills, and the information is understandable. One of the 16 highest paying customers said overhead information is not accessible and understandable. For example, this nonfederal customer and the Corps could not agree on whether overhead information requested by the customer had been provided, leaving the customer unable to understand Corps costs, including overhead information. The remaining 7 highest paying customers had no opinion on accessibility and/or understandability. While offering no opinion on one aspect of overhead information, such as accessibility, they generally offered a positive opinion on the other aspect, understandability. For example, one federal customer had no opinion on whether the information was accessible but said that the information was understandable because the Corps explains how it builds overhead into its projects during project meetings. Conversely, a nonfederal customer told GAO that he has requested and received overhead information from the Corps—stating that overhead information is accessible, but he offered no opinion on understanding it. Among customers GAO interviewed, there were common views about overhead information. Specifically, some customers indicated that overhead information is important, but that overall project costs are more important than overhead costs. They also said that good communication is important to understanding overhead information.

_____ United States Government Accountability Office

Contents

Letter		1
	Background	3
	The Corps Uses a MultiStep Process to Build Overhead Costs into Its Projects	7
	Customers' Views on Overhead Information	15
	Agency Comments and Our Evaluation	19

Appendix I	Objectives, Scope, and Methodology	20

Appendix II	Structured Interview Administered to U.S. Army Corps of Engineers' Customers	23

Appendix III	GAO Contact and Staff Acknowledgments	31

Tables		
	Table 1: Information on the U.S. Army Corps of Engineers' Federal and Nonfederal Customers	7
	Table 2: List of Highest Paying Customers Interviewed	22

Figures		
	Figure 1: Locations of the U.S. Army Corps of Engineers' Civil Works Divisions and Districts	4
	Figure 2: Overview of U.S. Army Corps of Engineers' Process for Building Overhead Costs into Projects	9
	Figure 3: Components of the Hourly Rate Charged to U.S. Army Corps of Engineers' Customers	13

GAO
U.S. GOVERNMENT ACCOUNTABILITY OFFICE

441 G St. N.W.
Washington, DC 20548

June 19, 2013

The Honorable David Vitter
Ranking Member
Committee on Environment and Public Works
United States Senate

Dear Senator Vitter:

The U.S. Army Corps of Engineers (Corps) is responsible for investigating, developing, and maintaining water resource projects and spends billions of dollars annually on a variety of projects in its Civil Works program.[1] As with private sector businesses, part of the cost of doing business with the Corps involves paying for overhead—costs that do not directly relate to a specific project or activity but more generally support agency operations. Examples of such costs include resource management, building security staff, rent, and information technology. Overhead costs are included in the amount that Congress appropriates for specific Corps projects and the amount customers pay for Corps' services. The Corps provides services to an array of customers including other Department of Defense units, other federal agencies, state and local governments, Indian tribes, and foreign governments. These services include engineering and construction services, environmental restoration and management services, research and development assistance, management of water and land related natural resources, relief and recovery work, and other management and technical services.

You asked us to review the Corps' process for building overhead costs into projects. This report examines (1) how the Corps builds overhead costs into its projects and (2) Corps customers' views on overhead information.

To determine how the Corps builds overhead costs into its projects, we reviewed Corps documentation regarding its overhead and billing processes including, among other things, overhead guidance for headquarters and the eight Corps divisions that conduct civil works

---

[1] In addition to the Civil Works program, the Corps has a Military program, which provides, among other things, engineering and construction services to other U.S. government agencies and foreign governments. This report only discusses the Civil Works program.

GAO-13-528 Army Corps Overhead Process

activities. We interviewed officials at Corps headquarters and two division and four district offices—selected based on geographic location—about the overhead process and information used to estimate, allocate, and bill overhead to projects. We did not evaluate the accuracy or legal sufficiency of the Corps' overhead formulas and calculations.[2] We received an agency demonstration of how the Corps' financial management system tracks overhead costs separately from other project costs, reviewed selected Corps customers' bills provided by the Corps and some Corps customers, reviewed Corps overhead documentation, interviewed Corps officials knowledgeable about how the Corps tracks and bills overhead costs, and interviewed selected Corps customers. To assess Corps customers' views on overhead, we interviewed the 16 highest paying federal and nonfederal customers in fiscal year 2012 for each of the eight Corps divisions that conduct civil works activities. Our questions covered the importance the customers place on obtaining overhead information, availability of and access to such information, and how understandable the customers find the overhead information the Corps provides. The interview results are not generalizable to all Corps civil works customers but provide illustrative examples for the 16 customers. In addition to these 16 customers, we interviewed 8 other Corps customers who represented geographic variation and different funding mechanisms to gather their views on the Corps' overhead information.[3] Appendix I contains more detailed information on our objectives, scope, and methodology and appendix II contains the questions from our interview with the 16 highest paying customers.

We conducted this performance audit from July 2012 to June 2013 in accordance with generally accepted government auditing standards. Those standards require that we plan and perform the audit to obtain sufficient, appropriate evidence to provide a reasonable basis for our findings and conclusions based on our audit objectives. We believe that the evidence obtained provides a reasonable basis for our findings and conclusions based on our audit objectives.

---

[2] This report is intended to provide a descriptive overview of the Corps' practices. It does not attempt to evaluate the legal sufficiency or propriety of these practices.

[3] Corps customers pay for Corps services through one of the following three funding mechanisms—on a reimbursable basis, on a cost share basis, and on a direct fund basis whereby the customer pays for Corps services in advance.

Background

The Corps is one of the world's largest public engineering, design, and construction management agencies. The Civil Works program employs about 23,000 full-time equivalents,[4] with staff in headquarters; 8 divisions, which were established generally according to watershed boundaries and are headed by a division commander, who is a military officer; and 38 districts nationwide.[5] The program covers hundreds of civil works projects nationwide and comprises water resource development activities, including flood risk management, navigation, recreation, and infrastructure and environmental stewardship. Headquarters and divisions generally establish policy and provide oversight, and districts implement projects. See fig. 1 for the locations of Corps civil works divisions and districts.

---

[4] A full-time equivalent consists of one or more employed individuals who collectively complete 2,080 work hours in a given year. Therefore, one full-time employee or two half-time employees equal one full-time equivalent.

[5] The Corps also has a number of centers that provide centralized services, such as financial services, and a number of Centers of Expertise that assist the Corps divisions and districts in the planning, design, and technical review of civil works projects. The Corps established the centers to consolidate expertise, improve consistency, reduce redundancy, and enhance institutional knowledge, among other things. For a full list of the Corps' Centers of Expertise, see http://www.usace.army.mil/about/centersofexpertise.aspx.

Figure 1: Locations of the U.S. Army Corps of Engineers' Civil Works Divisions and Districts

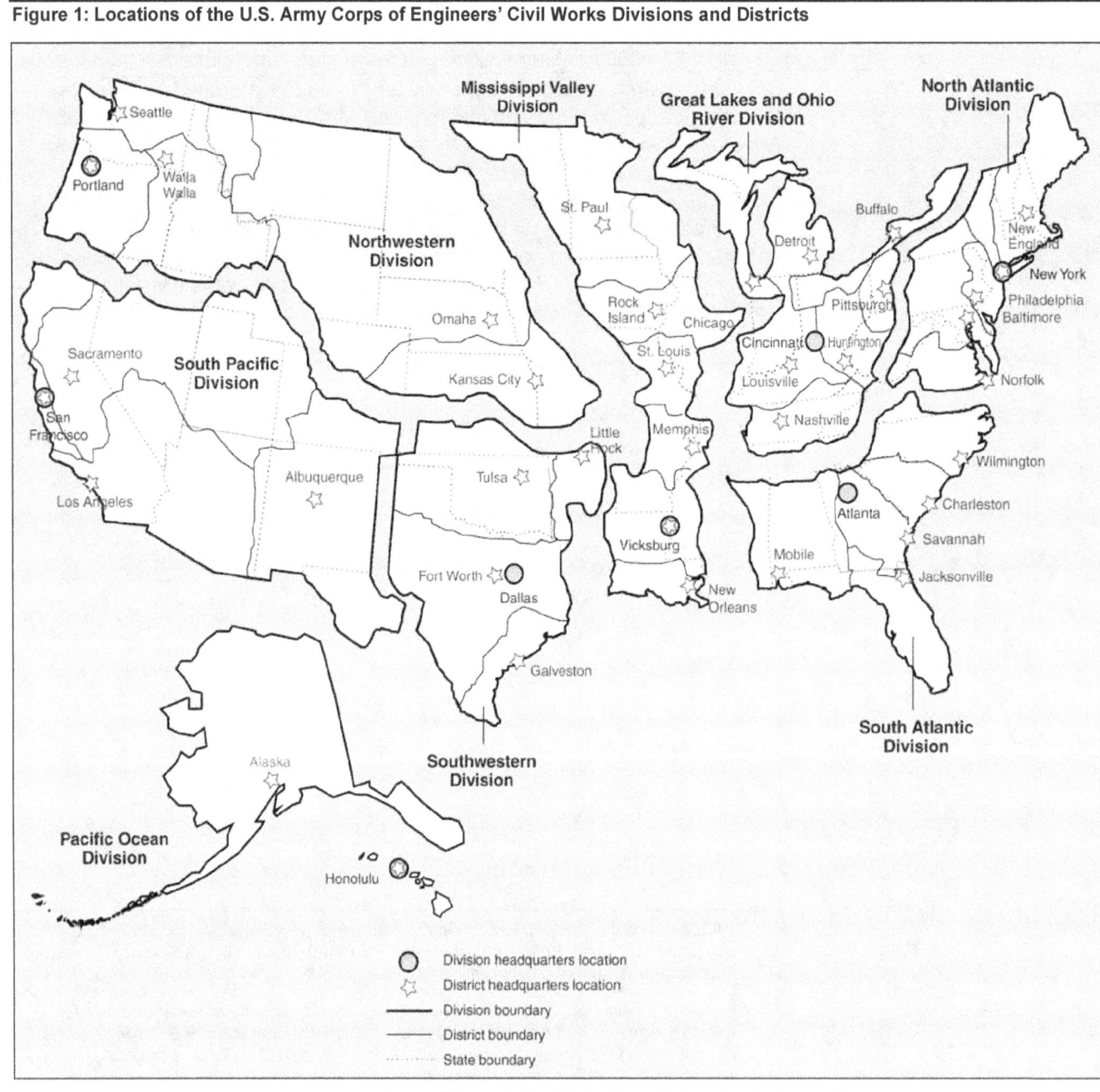

Sources: GAO representation of U.S. Army Corps of Engineers data; Map Resources (map).

GAO-13-528 Army Corps Overhead Process

More than 85 percent of Corps civil works staff work in the districts, which have a planning and executing role for Corps' projects. Each district office is headed by a district commander, who is also a military officer, and each district has a number of administrative and technical offices. Administrative offices, such as resource management, security, and general counsel, provide general administrative support. Technical offices, such as engineering, construction, and real estate, provide technical services to customers on specific projects.

Corps districts vary widely in the number of full-time equivalents they employ for civil works activities. Following are full-time equivalent data (in parentheses) for the two largest and two smallest districts, as well as two medium-sized districts, as reported by the Corps.

- The two largest districts: New Orleans (1,295) and Portland (1,155).
- Two medium-sized districts: Kansas City (530) and Fort Worth (515).
- The two smallest districts: Charleston (123) and Honolulu (64).

Only district overhead is charged to projects; headquarters and division overhead is not.[6] The Corps receives an appropriation that covers overhead expenses incurred by the Corps' headquarters and divisions. Districts, however, do not receive an appropriation to fund their overhead, so to cover those costs, districts must include overhead as part of project costs and bill those costs directly to customers.[7]

Districts use the Corps' revolving fund—a permanent appropriation established by the Civil Function Appropriations Act of 1954—to finance their overhead costs, then reimburse the fund with overhead payments received from project appropriations and customers.[8] In this way, the revolving fund, which maintains a number of accounts to which district staff charge their time, allows the financing of agency activities because the Corps charges for services and uses the proceeds to finance its spending, usually on a self-sustaining basis. Corps-wide policy includes a

---

[6] Certain centralized activities, such as information technology and human resource services, are directed by Corps headquarters and charged to districts.

[7] The Corps also has centers, such as the Huntsville Engineering Center, that do not receive an appropriation to fund their overhead.

[8] Pub. L. No. 83-153, 67 Stat. 197, 199 (1953), *codified as amended at* 33 U.S.C. §§ 576, 701b-10.

goal that each division's overhead account achieve a balance of zero at the end of each fiscal year.[9] Corps policy states that a balance within plus or minus 1 percent of actual expenses is considered the equivalent of a zero balance and, therefore, acceptable.[10]

The Corps receives the bulk of its funding from Congress. The Corps' fiscal year 2012 appropriations for the Civil Works program totaled about $6.7 billion—about $5 billion in regular appropriations and about $1.7 billion in disaster appropriations. The appropriation covering headquarters and division overhead expenses was $185 million. According to Corps officials, Congress provided about 73 percent of the Corps' civil works funding in fiscal year 2012. The remaining 27 percent—about $2.5 billion—was provided by the Corps' federal and nonfederal customers. Specifically, the Corps reported receiving about 17 percent of its fiscal year 2012 funding from federal customers on a reimbursable basis, about 6 percent from nonfederal customers on a cost share basis, and about 4 percent from federal customers on a direct fund basis, whereby the customer pays for Corps services in advance. Information on these federal and nonfederal customers is provided in table 1.

---

[9] U.S. Army Corps of Engineers, *Engineer Regulation 37-1-30, Change 4, February 28, 2007, Chapter 20: Revolving Fund Accounting for Departmental Overhead and Change 5, June 29, 2007, Chapter 21: Revolving Fund Accounting for General and Administrative Overhead.*

[10] To achieve this 1 percent goal, the Corps annually establishes quarterly targets, referred to as tolerance levels, for all divisions such that in the first quarter the division's balance should fall within plus or minus 4 percent of actual expenses, the third quarter within plus or minus 3 percent, the second quarter within plus or minus 2 percent, and finally within plus or minus 1 percent by the fourth quarter. Tolerance levels are calculated by multiplying expenses by the various percentages. For example, the first quarter tolerance would be a division's total expenses multiplied by 4 percent.

Table 1: Information on the U.S. Army Corps of Engineers' Federal and Nonfederal Customers

Customer type	Funding mechanism	Description of how the customer pays for Corps services	Description of how the customer is billed	Example of a customer and project
Federal	Reimbursements	Receives services and is later billed; pays for the entire cost of a project	Receives standard monthly invoices from the Corps	U.S. Environmental Protection Agency: design and construction of a Superfund site
	Direct fund	Pays for services in advance; shares in operation and maintenance and some capital improvements related to projects	Receives standard monthly invoices or statements from the Corps	Bonneville Power Administration: operations and maintenance of a hydroelectric power plant
Nonfederal	Cost share	Shares the cost of a project with the federal government; pays for services in advance through money, land, or work-in-kind	Billing is handled at the district level by the Corps project manager	Port Authority of New York and New Jersey: deepening of the New York Harbor

Source: GAO analysis U.S. Army Corps of Engineers information.

The Corps Uses a MultiStep Process to Build Overhead Costs into Its Projects

The Corps uses a multistep process to build overhead costs into projects. First, Corps policy establishes two categories of costs to calculate overhead. Second, the Corps calculates annual overhead rates for the two cost categories as part of its annual budget process. Third, the Corps bills projects for overhead costs based on the number of hours its staff charge to projects. Finally, the Corps monitors overhead costs and makes any necessary adjustments to overhead rates.

Corps Policy Establishes Two Categories of Costs to Calculate Overhead

Corps policy establishes two categories of costs to calculate overhead—general and administrative (G&A) overhead expenses associated with district administrative offices and technical overhead expenses associated with district technical offices.[11] These two categories serve as the foundation for building district overhead into projects. Corps policy defines G&A overhead as costs of a general or administrative nature, and all G&A overhead charges are based on a single rate per division.

---

[11] U.S. Army Corps of Engineers, *Engineer Regulation 37-1-30, Change 5, June 29, 2007, Chapter 21: Revolving Fund Accounting for General and Administrative Overhead* and *Engineer Regulation 37-1-30, Change 4, February 28, 2007, Chapter 20: Revolving Fund Accounting for Departmental Overhead.* The Corps also refers to technical overhead as departmental overhead.

Examples of G&A overhead include costs to run the district resource management or security offices, such as employee salaries and benefits and utilities.[12] Corps policy defines technical overhead as costs within a technical office—such as engineering or construction—that cannot be directly identified as part of or readily chargeable to a specific program or project. Examples of technical overhead are the hours spent by the head of the engineering office providing general supervision to engineering staff and the prorated portion of rent for the office space of the engineering staff. All technical overhead charges are based on four different rates per division—consolidated technical overhead, emergency management, operations, and regulatory.[13] Corps headquarters officials said that the four technical overhead rates reflect four distinct types of services rendered as follows:

- Consolidated technical overhead: This rate applies to state, local, and tribal governments working with the Corps to build new water resource projects.
- Emergency management: This rate applies to services rendered to the Federal Emergency Management Agency and state and local emergency management entities.
- Operations: This rate applies to state, local, and tribal governments receiving Corps services for the operation and maintenance of existing water resource projects.
- Regulatory: This rate applies to customers seeking Corps' permits to build on lands that might impact a wetland.

Using calculations based on the G&A rate and the applicable technical rates, districts build overhead costs into projects. This multistep process is outlined in fig. 2.

---

[12] G&A overhead includes costs associated with all of the following offices within a district: executive office, resource management/comptroller, public affairs, counsel, human resources, logistics management, equal employment opportunity, safety and occupational health, provost marshal/security, internal review, information management, contracting, real property inventory/reconciliations, union activities, marketing and outreach program activities, and results from operations.

[13] Consolidated technical overhead is a single rate that covers the overhead of the following district technical offices: construction, engineering, program/project management, real estate, planning, and contracting.

GAO-13-528 Army Corps Overhead Process

Figure 2: Overview of U.S. Army Corps of Engineers' Process for Building Overhead Costs into Projects

Corps policy establishes two categories of costs to calculate overhead.

Category 1:
General and administrative overhead

- Associated with district administrative offices, such as resource management and security.

- Consists of a single rate per division.

Category 2:
Technical overhead

- Associated with district technical offices, such as engineering and construction.

- Consists of four rates per division depending on the type of service rendered—consolidated technical overhead, emergency management, operations, and regulatory.[a]

Districts and divisions calculate overhead rates in the budget process.

- Each district technical and administrative office develops an operating budget with estimated overhead and submits it to district resource management.

- District resource management reviews and verifies operating budgets and prepares consolidated operating budget, including proposed overhead rates, for management review.

- District commander approves district operating budget.

- Districts submit proposed operating budgets to division.

- Division resource management reviews and verifies operating budgets and prepares consolidated operating budget, including proposed overhead rates, for management review.

- Division commander approves consolidated division operating budget and sets initial overhead rates for the year.

- Each overhead rate is determined by dividing the total estimated overhead costs for the category of overhead, such as general and administrative overhead, by the total estimated direct labor charged to projects.

Districts charge overhead to projects.

- Districts charge overhead to projects based on direct Corps labor.

- Overhead is not charged to hours worked by contracted labor.

- Total hourly rates used to charge projects include salary, employee benefits, general and administrative overhead, and technical overhead.

- Within each division, a single general and administrative overhead rate is charged to all projects, whereas technical overhead rates are applied depending on the technical office staff charging to the projects.

Districts, divisions, and headquarters monitor overhead.

- District resource management meets at least quarterly to review actual overhead expenses compared to budgeted overhead.

- Division resource management meets at least quarterly with district resource managers to review overhead rates and compare budgeted to actual overhead expenses.

- Headquarters holds a quarterly management review to assess the overall health of the revolving fund and ensure that divisions are within predetermined tolerance levels.[b]

- If overhead falls outside of the tolerance levels, divisions may adjust overhead rates, reduce spending, or provide customers with rebates.

Source: GAO analysis of U.S. Army Corps of Engineers information.

[a]Consolidated technical overhead is a single rate that covers the overhead of the following district technical offices: construction, engineering, program/project management, real estate, planning, and contracting.

[b]Congress established a revolving fund for the Corps in the Civil Function Appropriations Act of 1954 [Pub. L. No. 83-153, 67 Stat. 197, 1999 (1953), codified as amended at 33 U.S.C. §§ 576, 701b-10]. The fund allows the Corps to finance their overhead costs and then reimburse the fund with overhead amounts charged to and received from project appropriations and customers. The Corps established a goal that each division's overhead account achieve a zero balance at the end of each fiscal year. According to Corps Engineer Regulation 37-1-30: Chapter 20: Revolving Fund Accounting for Departmental Overhead, a balance within plus or minus 1 percent of actual expenses is considered the equivalent of a zero balance and, therefore, acceptable. To achieve this goal, the Corps annually establishes quarterly targets, referred to as tolerance levels, for all divisions such that in the first quarter the overhead balance should fall within plus or minus 4 percent of expenses, the second quarter within plus or minus 3 percent of expenses, the third quarter within plus or minus 2 percent of expenses, and finally within plus or minus 1 percent of expenses by the fourth quarter. Tolerance levels are calculated by multiplying expenses by the various percentages.

The Corps Calculates Annual Overhead Rates in Its Budget Process

Using the two categories of overhead defined in Corps policy as its starting point, each district administrative and technical office—with assistance from district budget staff—develops its own operating budget with estimated overhead for the year.[14] For administrative offices, officials estimate annual expenses, and most of their employees' time is charged as G&A overhead.[15] For technical offices, officials estimate annual revenues and expenses and also calculate the portion of technical office labor costs that will be charged directly to projects and the portion that will be charged to overhead. For example, a district's construction office operating budget might estimate that a project manager would spend 85 percent of his/her time charging directly to projects and spend the remaining 15 percent of the time charging to overhead for activities such as attending training and staff meetings. The administrative and technical offices' operating budgets also include costs for centrally provided services, such as information technology, as well as certain expenses with imposed caps, such as employee awards.

Once each district administrative and technical office completes its operating budget, the offices forward them to the district resource manager—who essentially serves as the chief financial officer for the district. The district resource manager reviews and verifies information from each office and then consolidates the submissions into a single district operating budget. A district advisory committee—known as the Program Budget Advisory Committee—reviews and recommends the budget to the district commander for approval. District operating budgets include proposed G&A and technical overhead rates for the district. Each overhead rate is determined by dividing the total estimated overhead costs for the category of overhead, such as G&A, by the total estimated direct labor expected to be charged to projects. For example, if a division estimated that the total G&A costs for all of its districts would be $200 million and estimated that the total district labor charges expected to be directly billed to projects would be $1 billion, then the division's G&A rate would be .20 ($200 million/$1 billion).

---

[14] As is the case with districts, Corps centers generally use the same process to develop operating budgets and estimate overhead.

[15] In some instances, G&A office employees charge their time directly to projects. For example, attorneys in the Office of Counsel providing services directly supporting project-related real estate activities will charge time to the project.

Once district commanders approve their district's operating budget, the district resource manager submits it to the division's resource manager who reviews and verifies information and then consolidates all of the district operating budgets into a division-wide operating budget with a proposed single set of G&A and technical overhead rates for the division. As is the case with the districts, a division advisory committee—known as the Regional Program Budget Advisory Committee—reviews and recommends the budget to the division commander for approval.[16] With limited exceptions, each division and district carries out this process annually, with the result being a single set of G&A and technical overhead rates charged each year for each Corps division.[17] Overhead rates may vary from division to division due to a number of factors, such as cost of living (e.g., rent is higher for the San Francisco District than the Albuquerque District) and composition of the workforce (e.g., a district with more senior level staff has higher salaries than a district with more junior level staff).

The Corps Bills Projects for Overhead Costs Based on the Hours Charged by Corps Staff for Work Performed

Once overhead rates have been calculated in the budget process, district staff perform their work and charge their time to various project and overhead revolving fund accounts. Those accounts are then reimbursed either through project appropriations or through bill payments from customers. Districts build overhead into projects using the rates provided in the approved division operating budget.[18] Overhead charges are applied to each project based on the hours charged by Corps staff;

[16] Prior to fiscal year 2007, overhead rates were set at the district level. Corps officials told us that because rates varied by district, customers were "shopping around" for the best rates leading to an inefficient system. Starting in fiscal year 2007, the Corps switched to setting overhead rates at the division level to provide for a more effective and efficient system. Specifically, having divisions set overhead rates provides more consistency for customers and allows districts within a division to more easily share resources, according to Corps officials.

[17] Corps policy states that regional rates do not apply to the Pacific Ocean Division, districts outside the contiguous United States, and centers, but that the standard overhead account structure is to be used in these locations. Therefore, each of these locations sets its own rates. Corps officials explained that this difference is due to geographic issues.

[18] Corps customers also pay for the cost of centralized services, such as information technology, and may also pay the costs of Corps centers. For example, on a given project, if a district uses the services of a Corps center of expertise, such as the Hydrologic Engineering Center, then the customer pays for the direct services of the center employee and the associated overhead of the center, in the same way they do for district staff charging directly to their projects.

overhead charges are not applied to hours worked by contracted labor, which can represent a substantial amount of work. The Corps reports that it contracts out most of its design work and all of its construction work to private sector entities, such as architectural and engineering firms and construction companies.

Within each division, a single G&A rate is applied to all projects, whereas technical rates are applied depending on the technical office staff charging to the projects. For example, for an employee in the regulatory office, overhead charges would include both the technical overhead regulatory rate, along with the G&A rate, for each hour charged to a specific project. Fig. 3 shows the components of the hourly rate charged to Corps' customers, along with an example of rates and associated costs.

Figure 3: Components of the Hourly Rate Charged to U.S. Army Corps of Engineers' Customers

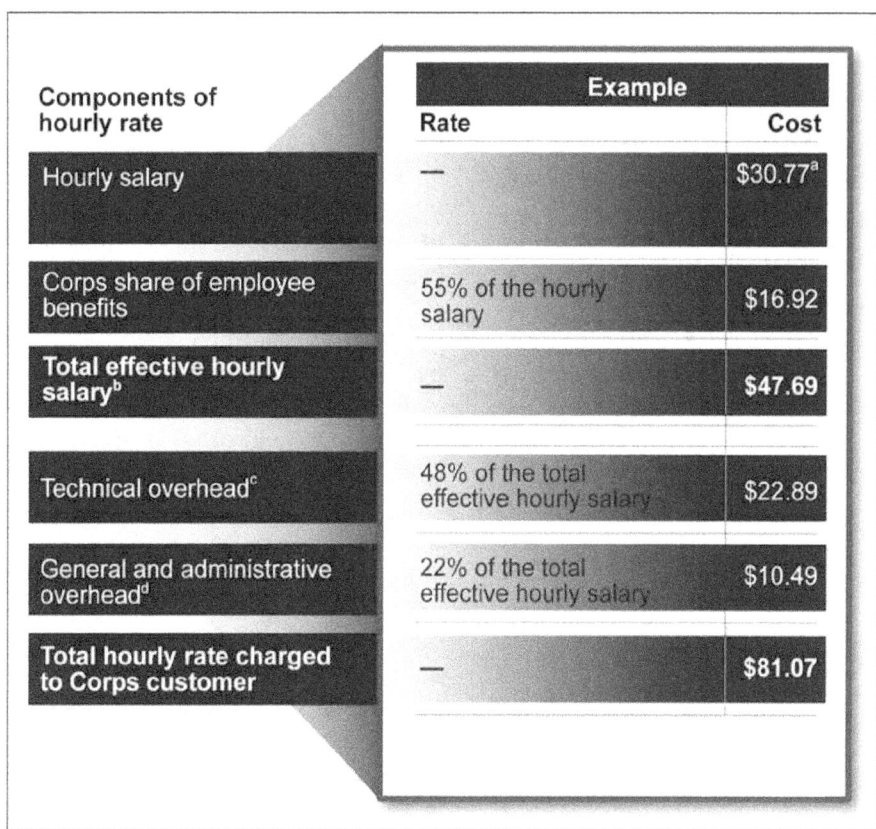

Components of hourly rate	Example	
	Rate	Cost
Hourly salary	—	$30.77[a]
Corps share of employee benefits	55% of the hourly salary	$16.92
Total effective hourly salary[b]	—	$47.69
Technical overhead[c]	48% of the total effective hourly salary	$22.89
General and administrative overhead[d]	22% of the total effective hourly salary	$10.49
Total hourly rate charged to Corps customer	—	$81.07

Source: GAO analysis of U. S. Army Corps of Engineers' data.

[a]This example assumes a full-time employee with a $64,000 annual salary divided by 2,080 hours of work per year.

[b]The Corps uses the term "total effective hourly salary" or "effective rate" to denote the cost per hour to fund a full-time employee's hourly salary plus the Corps' share of his or her benefits.

[c]Technical overhead is associated with the overhead of district technical offices, such as engineering and construction. Technical overhead rates are applied depending on the technical office staff charging to projects. For example, for an employee in the regulatory office, overhead charges would include both the technical overhead regulatory rate, along with the G&A rate, for each hour charged to a specific project.

[d]General and administrative overhead is associated with the overhead of district administrative offices, such as resource management and building security services. The general and administrative rate is applied to all projects.

According to Corps billing officials, customers who fund the Corps through a reimbursable or direct fund basis typically receive standard invoices or statements that include a breakout of these G&A and technical overhead costs. The billing for customers who share the costs of a project with the Corps, on the other hand, is handled by each individual district. According to the Corps, district project managers determine what is included in the billing information provided to customers.

The Corps Monitors Overhead Costs and Makes Any Necessary Adjustments

Periodically throughout the year, Corps headquarters, divisions, and districts monitor actual overhead expenses incurred, compare them with budgeted overhead estimates, and adjust rates charged to customers, if necessary, to help ensure the difference between budgeted and actual overhead is as close to zero as possible by the end of the fiscal year. Corps guidance calls for reviews of expenses and income no less than quarterly to determine whether budget projections and the existing overhead rates are on track. Corps officials told us that district staff, including those from resource management and budget, meet at least quarterly to review their actual expenditure of funds under a given budget. Corps officials further stated that division resource management and other officials meet at least quarterly with district staff to help ensure that actual expenses align with budgeted amounts. Moreover, Corps officials stated that, in a process known as the Directorate Management Review, Corps headquarters reviews overhead for all divisions on a quarterly basis to determine if there are any differences between budgeted and actual overhead that fall outside of targeted tolerance levels and the reasons for such differences. Based on these reviews, division commanders are responsible for ensuring that appropriate action is taken, such as adjusting overhead rates, reducing expenditures, or providing rebates to customers. Corps headquarters officials said that if the Corps takes in more revenue than was budgeted, this "income" is factored into the calculation of overhead rates for the next fiscal year, potentially resulting in lower overhead rates. The opposite is true if the Corps takes in less revenue than was budgeted.

The Corps is able to monitor overhead because it tracks overhead costs separately from other project costs in its financial management system by using specific accounting codes to identify overhead.[19] According to Corps officials, district staff are responsible for entering project activity data into the headquarters' financial management system using these

---

[19] The Corps uses its Corps of Engineers Financial Management System to perform key financial management functions supporting the Corps' military and civil works missions.

codes. We reviewed one district's expense reports and found that overhead costs were broken out separately from other project costs using categories such as training and rent. We also reviewed examples of the Corps' standard billings to customers and found that they all included a breakdown of G&A and technical overhead. According to Corps officials, tracking overhead costs is essential to meet the tolerance level goals set by the Corps for each fiscal quarter.

Customers' Views on Overhead Information

Customers' views on whether overhead information is accessible and understandable varied. Half of the 16 highest paying customers we interviewed said overhead information is generally accessible and understandable; 1 of the 16 said overhead information is not accessible and understandable; and the remaining 7 had no opinion on accessibility and/or understandability. For those customers who offered no opinion on one aspect of overhead information, such as accessibility, they generally offered a positive opinion on the other aspect of information, understandability. Like these 16 customers, the views of the 8 other Corps customers we interviewed varied. In addition, customers we interviewed provided some common views on overhead information, stating that overhead information is important, but that overall project costs are more important than overhead costs. They also emphasized the importance of good communication with the Corps to understanding overhead information.

Customers' Views Varied on Whether Overhead Information Is Accessible and Understandable

Customers' views fell into three broad categories: (1) overhead information is generally accessible and understandable, (2) overhead information is not accessible and understandable, and (3) no opinion on whether overhead information is accessible and/or understandable.

Overhead Information is Generally Accessible and Understandable

In our interviews with the highest paying federal and nonfederal customers in each of the 8 Corps divisions in fiscal year 2012, 8 of 16 customers said overhead information is generally accessible and understandable. For example, one nonfederal customer said overhead information is accessible and easy to understand because the information is included in its project agreement with the Corps, which is signed prior to the start of a project. Another federal customer we interviewed said that the Corps provides overhead information in monthly bills and that this information was also understandable. Moreover, that customer pointed out that, if more overhead information was needed, she could ask the Corps for such information and the Corps would provide it.

While half of the highest paying customers said overhead information is generally accessible and understandable, seven of them noted that understanding overhead information required some work. For example, one federal customer said it sometimes takes several e-mail exchanges with the Corps to understand overhead terminology. While generally understanding overhead information, this customer said he would like to review bills with the Corps to better understand what is charged as overhead on a project. Another federal customer said that a customer must be familiar with the Corps and its processes to understand the overhead billing. Moreover, two federal customers said that they do not have a complete understanding of overhead charges because the Corps does not provide a detailed breakdown of overhead costs throughout the course of the project.

Overhead Information is Not Accessible and Not Understandable

One of the 16 highest paying customers said that overhead information is not accessible and therefore was unable to assess whether it is understandable. This nonfederal customer said that a Corps district had denied a request for overhead rates and a detailed breakdown of overhead costs by Corps employee. Asked about this, district officials said they had reached an agreement with the customer to provide detailed overhead information and provided a sample report demonstrating the overhead information, but that the customer did not respond to the Corps' request to accept this information. However, this customer disagreed and said the overhead information request is still unresolved, making it difficult to manage ongoing projects without knowing how the Corps spends project funds or what it charges for overhead. Neither the customer nor the Corps provided us written documentation substantiating the resolution of the overhead information request.

In addition to our interviews with the highest paying customers, we interviewed eight additional customers. Two of these customers—customers we identified as potentially having concerns about the Corps' overhead process—said the Corps provides them with little or no overhead information and that what overhead information they do receive is difficult to understand.[20] One of those customers told us that the Corps had not provided overhead information when it was requested. Corps officials said that although they do not have a formal written policy on

[20] See appendix I for additional information on how these customers were selected.

providing overhead information to customers, overhead information is available to any customer upon request.

No Opinion on Whether Overhead Information is Accessible and/or Understandable

Seven of the 16 highest paying customers did not have an opinion on accessibility and/or understandability of overhead information. Those that offered no opinion on one aspect, such as accessibility, generally offered a positive opinion on the other aspect, understandability.

- Two of the seven highest paying customers did not express an opinion on whether overhead information is accessible and understandable. One nonfederal customer told us that he did not request overhead information from the Corps, in part because he accepts the Corps' overhead rates and charges as a given. Because he does not request overhead information, this customer could not comment on whether overhead information is accessible and understandable. Another nonfederal customer said he was more concerned about the overall costs of the project than the overhead charges and, therefore, had no opinion on the accessibility and understandability of overhead information. In additional interviews with eight federal and nonfederal customers, one nonfederal customer was not concerned about overhead information, explaining that he agreed to project costs up front with the Corps and from that point on both parties are responsible for their share of the costs.

- Three of the seven highest paying customers stated that overhead information is accessible but had no opinion on whether the information is understandable. For example, one nonfederal customer said that overhead information is available, if needed, but this customer does not request such information because he has a good working relationship with the Corps and trusts that the Corps is building overhead into projects appropriately. This customer did not, however, offer an opinion on whether overhead information is understandable. Another nonfederal customer told us that he has requested and received overhead information from the Corps, but he offered no opinion on understanding overhead information.

- Two of the seven highest paying customers expressed no opinion on the accessibility of overhead information but stated such information was understandable. For example, one federal customer said that while he has not requested overhead information, the Corps explained how it builds overhead into its projects during project meetings and that he understood this information. Another federal customer said that while he has no opinion on the accessibility of information, he is able to understand overhead using his agencies' in-house expertise.

GAO-13-528 Army Corps Overhead Process

Customers Provided Additional Views on Overhead Information

Of the 24 customers we interviewed, a number expressed common views regarding overhead information. Specifically, these included:

- *Overhead information is important.* Most customers told us that overhead information is important and that knowing those costs up front is also important. Specifically, some customers told us that knowing overhead costs up front helps their organizations determine whether costs are reasonable before starting a project with the Corps. In some cases, customers said they could secure services from a source other than the Corps, so overhead information is important in determining whether to select the Corps to manage their projects. Some customers said due to the direct impact of overhead costs on the project's total cost, knowing those costs up front allows their organizations to plan project funding appropriately.

- *Overall project cost is more important than overhead costs.* Some customers we interviewed said they were more interested in the overall project cost than specific overhead charges. Ten of 16 highest paying customers said they had requested a detailed breakdown of project costs including overhead charges. This was the most frequent type of information requested from the Corps, according to our interviews. In substantiating what we learned from customers, Corps headquarters officials told us that customers are more interested in the overall project cost than overhead costs, and customers typically do not ask for overhead information. Specifically, Corps officials said that customers who pay for Corps services on a reimbursable basis—typically federal agencies—receive regular bills or statements that include a breakdown of overhead charges and, therefore, may be more aware of overhead costs and any rate changes.

- *Good communication is important to understanding overhead information.* Four of the highest paying customers that expressed positive views on the accessibility and understandability of overhead information said their organizations have good communication and working relationship with the Corps. For example, one of the nonfederal highest paying customers said that his organization communicates frequently with the Corps and has developed a positive working relationship with the Corps over decades that could serve as a model for other organizations. Three of the highest paying customers added that communication such as discussions of overhead at regular project meetings or a fact sheet would help them better understand overhead information.

Agency Comments and Our Evaluation

We provided a draft of this report for review and comment to the Department of Defense. Because the report does not contain any recommendations, the department did not provide written comments. The department did provide technical comments, which we incorporated into the report as appropriate.

As agreed with your office, unless you publicly announce the contents of this report earlier, we plan no further distribution until 7 days from the report date. At that time, we will send copies to the Secretary of Defense, the Chief of Engineers and Commanding General of the U.S. Army Corps of Engineers, the appropriate congressional committees, and other interested parties. In addition, the report will be available at no charge on the GAO website at http://www.gao.gov.

If you or your staff members have any questions about this report, please contact me at (202) 512-3841 or fennella@gao.gov. Contact points for our Offices of Congressional Relations and Public Affairs may be found on the last page of this report. GAO staff who made key contributions to this report are listed in appendix III.

Sincerely yours,

Anne-Marie Fennell
Director, Natural Resources and Environment

Appendix I: Objectives, Scope, and Methodology

Our objectives were to examine (1) how the U.S. Army Corps of Engineers (Corps) builds overhead costs into its projects and (2) Corps customers' views on overhead information.

To address the first objective, we reviewed Corps documentation regarding its overhead determination and billing processes including, among other things, overhead briefings, budget memos, and guidance from headquarters and the eight Corps divisions that conduct civil works projects. We interviewed officials at Corps headquarters, two of eight division offices (North Atlantic and Northwest), and 4 of 38 district offices (Baltimore, New Orleans, Portland, and Vicksburg) about the overhead process and information used to estimate, allocate, and bill overhead to projects. We selected these offices to ensure geographic variation. We interviewed eight Corps officials from four Corps districts knowledgeable about the overhead process, including estimating overhead costs and setting overhead rates. Specifically, we interviewed four randomly selected Corps resource managers—a district's chief financial officer who oversees the formulation of a district's operating budget including district overhead rates—as well as the heads of four Corps technical offices who oversee the estimates of overhead by employee. We received a demonstration on how the Corps' financial management system is designed to track overhead separately from other project costs, reviewed examples of Corps billings to customers provided by the Corps and some Corps customers, reviewed Corps financial management system documentation, interviewed selected Corps customers, and interviewed Corps officials knowledgeable about how the Corps tracks and bills overhead costs. While we generally reviewed the Corps' methodology to develop overhead rates, we did not evaluate the accuracy or legal sufficiency of the Corps' overhead formulas and calculations.[1] For civil works projects, we only focused on general and administrative and technical overhead. Although the Corps charges overhead for military and civil works projects, we did not review how the Corps charges overhead to military projects.

In addressing the second objective, we interviewed six Corps customers from the North Atlantic and Northwest Divisions, respectively, to gather their views on the Corps' overhead process, including whether overhead

---

[1] This report is intended to provide a descriptive overview of the Corps' practices. It does not attempt to evaluate the legal sufficiency or propriety of these practices.

information is accessible and understandable. Specifically, we
interviewed Bonneville Power Administration, Bureau of Reclamation,
Environmental Protection Agency, Maryland Department of Natural
Resources, Wicomico County Department of Public Works, and a military
customer. We selected these customers to provide geographic variation
and to ensure representation of at least one customer from each type of
funding mechanism—reimbursable, cost share, and direct fund basis. The
views of these customers are not generalizable to all Corps civil works
customers but provide illustrative examples for the six customers. To help
us understand the nature of concerns certain customers had expressed
about the Corps' overhead to congressional staff and to design a
structured interview protocol, we selected two additional customers to
interview—Southeast Louisiana Floodplain Authority–East and Southeast
Louisiana Floodplain Authority–West. We randomly selected these
customers from an extensive list of potential customers who had
previously expressed concerns to congressional staff. Although these
customers added to the geographic variation and to the variety of funding
mechanisms represented, their views do not represent the views of Corps
civil works customers generally, but rather, are indicative of customers
that had previously expressed concerns to congressional staff. We then
sought to determine views from a broader group of customers by
conducting structured interviews with the 16 highest paying federal and
highest paying nonfederal customers in fiscal year 2012—one in each
category from all 8 Corps divisions. The names of the 16 customers we
interviewed are listed in table 2. Our questions covered the importance
customers place on obtaining overhead information, availability of and
access to such information, and the extent to which the overhead
information they receive is understandable. A detailed list of structured
interview questions is presented in appendix II. The structured interview
results are not generalizable to all Corps civil works customers but
provide illustrative examples for the 16 customers. We conducted
structured phone interviews from January 2013 to March 2013, and we
completed 16 of 16 interviews. Prior to interviewing the 16 customers, we
pretested the structured interview with two customers to ensure that the
questions were relevant, free of bias, clearly stated, and easy to
understand and, based on those results, made adjustments to the
structured interview as necessary. To ensure tabulated responses were
accurate, we checked data recorded during structured interviews. We
also spoke with Corps officials regarding customer views on the
accessibility and understandability of overhead information.

Table 2: List of Highest Paying Customers Interviewed

	Customer	Federal / nonfederal	Corps Division
1.	American Samoa Government	Nonfederal	Pacific Ocean
2.	Coastal Restoration and Protection Authority	Nonfederal	Mississippi Valley
3.	County of Los Angeles, Department of Beach and Harbors	Nonfederal	South Pacific
4.	Logan County Commission	Nonfederal	Lakes and Rivers
5.	NAF Financial Services	Nonfederal	South Atlantic
6.	Port Authority of New York and New Jersey	Nonfederal	North Atlantic
7.	Port of Corpus Christi Authority	Nonfederal	Southwest
8.	State of Idaho	Nonfederal	Northwest
9.	U.S. Department of Commerce, National Oceanic and Atmospheric Administration	Federal	Pacific Ocean
10.	U.S. Department of Homeland Security, Federal Emergency Management Agency	Federal	Mississippi Valley
11.	U.S. Department of Homeland Security, U.S. Customs and Border Protection	Federal	Southwest
12.	U.S. Department of Veterans Affairs	Federal	Lakes and Rivers
13.	U.S. Department of Veterans Affairs	Federal	South Atlantic
14.	U.S. Department of Veterans Affairs	Federal	South Pacific
15.	U.S. Environmental Protection Agency	Federal	North Atlantic
16.	U.S. Environmental Protection Agency	Federal	Northwest

Source: U.S. Army Corps of Engineers.

We conducted this performance audit from July 2012 to June 2013 in accordance with generally accepted government auditing standards. Those standards require that we plan and perform the audit to obtain sufficient, appropriate evidence to provide a reasonable basis for our findings and conclusions based on our audit objectives. We believe that the evidence obtained provides a reasonable basis for our findings and conclusions based on our audit objectives.

Appendix II: Structured Interview Administered to U.S. Army Corps of Engineers' Customers

We conducted structured interviews with 16 Corps customers that the Corps identified as the highest paying federal and highest paying nonfederal customers in fiscal year 2012—one in each category from all eight Corps divisions. This appendix presents the detailed list of the structured interview questions we asked.

SECTION 1: BACKGROUND

1. Please briefly describe your current position at your organization, including the number of years you have held that position.

2. Now we'd like you to generally describe your experience working with the Corps within the last 3 years. Specifically:

   a. About how many years has your organization been a customer of the Corps?

   b. How many active projects have you had during this period?

      Interview instruction: Base the next question off of the answer in part a. If they said they had 2-3 active projects, than read the question as is. If they say they had 10-20 or more projects, than ask them to discuss maybe the 2-3 largest ones.

   c. Could you briefly describe these projects? In doing so, we're looking for the services the Corps provided to those projects and the current state of the project, such as design or construction.

SECTION 2: IMPORTANCE OF AND REQUESTING OVERHEAD INFORMATION

Thinking of the active projects we just discussed over our 3-year time frame, I'd now like to walk you through a series of specific questions on Corps overhead. If you need me to repeat anything, please don't hesitate to stop me.

3. How important, if at all, are each of the following types of overhead information for your organization in conducting business with the Corps? *I will read you a list of 5 types of information and for each of these types of information, please tell me if it is very important, somewhat important, or not important.*

		Very important	Somewhat important	Not important	Not applicable	Don't know
a.	The total overhead cost for your project	☐	☐	☐	☐	☐
b.	The overhead rate applied to your project	☐	☐	☐	☐	☐
c.	The methodology used to calculate overhead rates	☐	☐	☐	☐	☐
d.	Notice of changes in overhead rates	☐	☐	☐	☐	☐
e.	A detailed breakdown of charges for your project, including overhead	☐	☐	☐	☐	☐
f.	Other: Please describe:	☐	☐	☐	☐	☐

Interview instruction: If the respondent answers not applicable and/or don't know in question 3 (i.e., how important are each of the following types of overhead information), then skip question 3a. Otherwise, proceed with question 3a.

3a. Why is overhead information important for your organization in conducting business with the Corps?

4. **During the past 3 years, did you request any of the following types of overhead information from the Corps?** I will read you a list of the same five types of information and for each of these types of information, please tell me if you requested it or if you did not request it.

		Yes, requested	No, did not request	Not applicable	Don't know
a.	The total overhead cost for your project	☐	☐	☐	☐
b.	The overhead rate applied to your project	☐	☐	☐	☐
c.	The methodology used to calculate overhead rates	☐	☐	☐	☐
d.	Notice of changes in overhead rates	☐	☐	☐	☐
e.	A detailed breakdown of charges for your project, including overhead	☐	☐	☐	☐
f.	Other: Please describe: _____	☐	☐	☐	☐

Interview instruction: If the respondent answers no in questions 3 and 4 (i.e., overhead information is not important to them and they have not requested it), than skip question 5. Otherwise, proceed with question 5.

5. During the past 3 years, have you received enough of each of the following types of overhead information for your organization in conducting business with the Corps? *I will read you a list of the same five types of information and for each of these types of information, please tell me if you have received enough, some but not enough, or none for your purpose.*

		Received enough	Received some but not enough	Received none	Not applicable	Don't know
a.	The total overhead cost for your project	☐	☐	☐	☐	☐
b.	The overhead rate applied to your project	☐	☐	☐	☐	☐
c.	The methodology used to calculate overhead rates	☐	☐	☐	☐	☐
d.	Notice of changes in overhead rates	☐	☐	☐	☐	☐
e.	A detailed breakdown of charges for your project, including overhead	☐	☐	☐	☐	☐
f.	Other: Please describe: _____	☐	☐	☐	☐	☐

SECTION 3: IMPACT QUESTIONS

<u>Interview instruction</u>: Base the asking of questions 6 and 7 on the answer to question 5. You may skip one or both depending on the answers provided. Also, repeat their answers to question 5 in asking each question.

6. In the previous question, you said that you "received some but not enough" or "received none" of a particular type of overhead information. What impact, if any, did this have on your organization? And please explain why.

7. Referring again to your response to question five, you said that you "received enough" of a particular type of overhead information. What impact, if any, did the availability of overhead information have on your organization? And please explain why.

8. For the active projects within the last 3 years, do you recall the Corps providing general overhead information prior to signing an initial project contract or agreement? Y/N Please explain.

<u>Interview instruction</u>: If the respondent answers no to question 8, skip questions 9 and 10. If yes, proceed in asking 9 and 10.

9. **To what extent were you satisfied with the overhead information the Corps' provided prior to the signing of the initial project contract or agreement?**

	Very satisfied	Somewhat satisfied	Not satisfied	Not applicable	Don't know
_____ —	☐	☐	☐	☐	☐

10. Please explain why you were or were not satisfied with the overhead information you received prior to signing an initial project contract or agreement.

SECTION 4: OVERALL OPINION OF ACCESS TO AND EASE OF UNDERSTANDING OVERHEAD INFORMATION

11. Given all of the responses to the questions I've already asked, how access ble is information on Corps overhead?

	Available and easy to access	Available but hard to access	Not available	Not applicable	Don't know
_____ _	☐	☐	☐	☐	☐

Interview instruction: If the respondent answers not applicable and/or don't know in question 11 (i.e., how available is overhead information), then skip question 11a. Otherwise, proceed with question 11a.

11a. Why is overhead information either available and easy to access, available, but hard to access or not available?

12. Given all of the responses to the questions I've already asked, how understandable is information on Corps overhead?

	Easy to understand	Understanda ble but requires some work	Not understandab le	Not applicable	Don't know
_____ _	☐	☐	☐	☐	☐

Interview instruction: If the respondent answers not applicable and/or don't know in question 12 (i.e., how available is overhead information), then skip question 12a. Otherwise, proceed with question 13.

12a. Why is overhead information either easy to understand, understandable, but requires some work, or not understandable?

13. **During the past 3 years, in which of the following ways has the Corps communicated overhead information on your current active project(s)?** *I will read you a list of five ways in which the Corps may have communicated this information and for each way, please tell me if you received it or you did not receive it.*

		Yes, I received overhead information in this manner	No, I did not receive overhead information in this manner	Not applicable	Don't know
a.	Memoranda of Agreement/Project Partnership Agreement/Contract	☐	☐	☐	☐
b.	Project update meetings with Corps project manager	☐	☐	☐	☐
c.	Invoices/billing	☐	☐	☐	☐
d.	Overhead briefing	☐	☐	☐	☐
e.	Overhead fact sheet	☐	☐	☐	☐
f.	Other – please specify _____	☐	☐	☐	☐

SECTION 5: OPEN ENDED QUESTIONS

14. Please describe any concerns you have had about Corps' overhead charges. In your answer, please any general concerns with overhead charges and any specific examples.

15. How did the Corps help resolve your concerns about overhead charges?

16. Do you think the Corps can make any improvement to help ensure information on the overhead costs you are paying is available to you and easy to access? Y/N Please explain.

17. Do you think the Corps can make any improvement to help ensure information on the overhead costs you are paying is easy for you to understand? Y/N Please explain.

18. Do you have suggestions for any other individuals or organizations we should consider reaching out to in reviewing the Corps' overhead process? Y/N. If yes, please provide the contact information.

19. Do you have any other comments about the Corps' overhead process? Y/N. If yes, please describe.

Appendix III: GAO Contact and Staff Acknowledgments

GAO Contact	Anne-Marie Fennell, (202) 512-3841 or fennella@gao.gov
Staff Acknowledgments	In addition to the individual named above, Vondalee R. Hunt (Assistant Director), Mark A. Braza, Nkenge Gibson, Mark Keenan, Jeanette Soares, and Jack Warner made key contributions to this report. Cheryl Arvidson, Arkelga Braxton, Peter B. Grinnell, Armetha Liles, and Vasiliki Theodoropoulos also made important contributions to this report.

GAO's Mission	The Government Accountability Office, the audit, evaluation, and investigative arm of Congress, exists to support Congress in meeting its constitutional responsibilities and to help improve the performance and accountability of the federal government for the American people. GAO examines the use of public funds; evaluates federal programs and policies; and provides analyses, recommendations, and other assistance to help Congress make informed oversight, policy, and funding decisions. GAO's commitment to good government is reflected in its core values of accountability, integrity, and reliability.
Obtaining Copies of GAO Reports and Testimony	The fastest and easiest way to obtain copies of GAO documents at no cost is through GAO's website (http://www.gao.gov). Each weekday afternoon, GAO posts on its website newly released reports, testimony, and correspondence. To have GAO e-mail you a list of newly posted products, go to http://www.gao.gov and select "E-mail Updates."
Order by Phone	The price of each GAO publication reflects GAO's actual cost of production and distribution and depends on the number of pages in the publication and whether the publication is printed in color or black and white. Pricing and ordering information is posted on GAO's website, http://www.gao.gov/ordering.htm. Place orders by calling (202) 512-6000, toll free (866) 801-7077, or TDD (202) 512-2537. Orders may be paid for using American Express, Discover Card, MasterCard, Visa, check, or money order. Call for additional information.
Connect with GAO	Connect with GAO on Facebook, Flickr, Twitter, and YouTube. Subscribe to our RSS Feeds or E-mail Updates. Listen to our Podcasts. Visit GAO on the web at www.gao.gov.
To Report Fraud, Waste, and Abuse in Federal Programs	Contact: Website: http://www.gao.gov/fraudnet/fraudnet.htm E-mail: fraudnet@gao.gov Automated answering system: (800) 424-5454 or (202) 512-7470
Congressional Relations	Katherine Siggerud, Managing Director, siggerudk@gao.gov, (202) 512-4400, U.S. Government Accountability Office, 441 G Street NW, Room 7125, Washington, DC 20548
Public Affairs	Chuck Young, Managing Director, youngc1@gao.gov, (202) 512-4800 U.S. Government Accountability Office, 441 G Street NW, Room 7149 Washington, DC 20548